GOD'S CREATIVE POWER®
FOR GRANDPARENTS

By
Beverly Ann Capps

Copyright

Contents

Forward

The Bible is one of our most important connections to God's will for us.

God's Creative Power® For Grandparents

As a grandparent you want to partake in the spiritual training of your grandchildren. One of the most important aspects of training children, is understanding that spiritual principles are conceived in the heart or spirit of a human being, not in the intellect. There are many adults who have intellectual knowledge of God's Word, but have no faith in that Word to produce spiritually in their own life. Babies are born with a spirit alive unto God and have full capability to receive spiritual laws into their hearts from birth. It is never too early to start confessing the Word of God over your grandchildren! They do not have to be present for you to affect their spiritual health. Speak the truth of God's Word over them daily!

God's Creative Power®

God's Word is the blueprint for what we can be through Christ. Through the Bible, God gives us scriptural truths about who we are in him. Through faith in his Word we see scriptural truths become truth in our lives. Faith is built through accepting the Word of God as fact in our lives and it becomes a reality for us. The blueprint on which we build our lives <u>is</u>

God's Word. God's Word spoken out of our mouth is creative power. Life and death are in the power of the tongue.

Calling Things That Are Not

God's method is through calling things that be not as though they were. God called Gideon a mighty man of valor when he was hiding behind the winepress. He did not appear to be a "mighty Man of Valor" at the time, but God spoke those words before it came to pass. You must hear and speak these truths before they are conceived in the spirit and become a reality. God called Abraham "Father of Nations" before Sarah had conceived. "Father of Nations" eventually became a reality for Abraham. We are to be imitators of God, we are created in His image and He spoke things into existence. The same principle operates in us.

Faith Comes By Hearing

Romans 10:17 "So then Faith cometh by hearing and hearing by the Word of God."

You must realize that the provisions Christ made for us through the atonement will only become a reality to us when we accept His Word over every circumstance. While just saying these scriptural truths will not make them reality, saying them is involved in causing faith to come. It is faith in God's Word that will overcome every circumstance.

We believe what we hear ourselves say. This is true both negatively and positively. As you begin speaking God's Word over your grandchildren you will develop your faith that God's Word is working in their lives. Make sure the words you are speaking at all times, are in line with Jesus' words!

We have included confessions for children as well, so that if they are with you, they can participate in applying spiritual truths in their lives. Make it fun for them so they enjoy that special time of spiritual training with you. Don't get in bondage to a schedule and make it a point of contention. It should be enjoyable for you and for them! Many of them will be able to quote the confessions from memory eventually, and you will be amazed at how quickly their spirits develop in spiritual principles.

Enjoy your time with your grandchildren!

Beverly Ann Capps

SCRIPTURE

Psalms 107:1

O give thanks unto the Lord, for he is good: for his mercy endureth for ever.

Hebrews 13:15

By him therefore let us offer the sacrifice of praise to God continually, that is, the fruit of our lips giving thanks to his name.

THANKSGIVING

My grandchildren give thanks unto the Lord for He is good and His Mercy endureth forever. My grandchildren are full of the knowledge of God and of thanksgiving for God and His Word. My grandchildren are full of thanksgiving.

SCRIPTURE

Ephesians 4:32

And be ye kind one to another, tenderhearted, forgiving one another, even as God for Christ's sake hath forgiven you.

Luke 6:38

Give, and it shall be given unto you; good measure, pressed down, and shaken together, and running over, shall men give into your bosom. For with the same measure that ye mete withal it shall be measured to you again.

KINDNESS

My grandchildren are kind to others, tenderhearted, forgiving others as God has forgiven them. As they give kindness unto others it is given back unto them, good measure, pressed down, shaken together and running over.

SCRIPTURE

Luke 10:27

And he answering said, Thou shalt love the Lord thy God with all thy heart, and all thy soul, and with all thy strength, and with all thy mind; and thy neighbor as thyself.

LOVE

My grandchildren love the Lord with all of their heart, with all their soul, and with all their strength, and with all their mind. The love of God is shed abroad in their hearts by the Holy Spirit that dwells within them.

SCRIPTURE

Philippians 4:6-8

Be careful for nothing; but in everything by prayer and supplication with thanksgiving let your requests be made known unto God. And the peace of God which passeth all understanding, shall keep your hearts and minds through Christ Jesus. Finally, brethren, whatsoever things are true, whatsoever things are honest, whatsoever things are just, whatsoever things are pure, whatsoever things are lovely, whatsoever things are of good report; if there be any virtue and if there be any praise, think on these things.

PRAISE

My grandchildren are full of praise because the goodness of God leads them to repentance. Their minds are filled with things that are true, honest, just, lovely, and of good report. They are obedient to the spirit of God and full of His Word and His Spirit.

SCRIPTURE

James 1:17

Every good gift and every perfect gift is from above, and cometh down from the Father of lights, with whom is no variableness, neither shadow of turning.

Joshua 1:8

This book of the law shall not depart out of thy mouth; but thou shalt meditate therein day and night, that thou mayest observe to do according to all that is written therein: for then thou shalt make thy way prosperous, and then thou shalt have good success.

Deuteronomy 28:8

The Lord shall command the blessing upon thee in thy storehouses, and in all that thou settest thine hand unto; and he shall bless thee in the land which the Lord thy God giveth thee.

BLESSING

My grandchildren are a good and perfect gift from God. They are full of gentleness, goodness, and faith. Everything they set their hands to do will prosper.

SCRIPTURE

Proverbs 18:10

The name of the Lord is a strong tower: the righteous run into it, and is safe.

Psalms 91:9-12

Because thou hast made the Lord, which is my refuge, even the most High, thy habitation; There shall no evil befall thee, neither shall any plague come nigh thy dwelling. For he shall give his angels charge over thee to keep thee in all thy ways. They shall bear thee up in their hands, lest thou dash thy foot against a stone.

SAFETY

My grandchildren are safe because the name of the Lord is a strong tower and they run into it and are safe. God has given his angels charge over them to keep them in all of their ways. He will satisfy them with long life.

SCRIPTURE

Philippians 4:6-7

Be careful for nothing; but in everything by prayer and supplication with thanksgiving let your requests be made known unto God. And the peace of God which passeth all understanding, shall keep your hearts and minds through Christ Jesus.

PEACE

Great is the peace of my grandchildren because they are taught of the Lord. The peace of God that passes all understanding guards their hearts and their minds through Jesus. My grandchildren are peaceful, for they are the blessed of the Lord.

SCRIPTURE

Hebrews 4:12

For the word of God is quick, and powerful, and sharper than any twoedged sword, piercing even to the dividing asunder of soul and spirit, and of the joints and marrow, and is a discerner of the thoughts and intents of the heart.

John 16:13-14

Howbeit when he, the Spirit of truth, is come, he will guide you into all truth; for he shall not speak of himself; but whatsoever he shall hear, that shall he speak; and he will shew you things to come. He shall glorify me: for he shall receive of mine, and shall shew it unto you.

TRUTH

My grandchildren are obedient to God's Word. The Word of God is sharp and powerful and divides between the soul and the spirit. The spirit of God inside my grandchildren gives them divine knowledge and guidance in all things.

SCRIPTURE

I Peter 2:24

Who his own self bare our sins in his own body on the tree, that we, being dead to sins, should live unto righteousness: by whose stripes ye were healed.

Proverbs 3:7-8

Be not wise in thine own eyes: fear the Lord, and depart from evil. It shall be health to thy navel, and marrow to thy bones.

HEALTH

My grandchildren were healed
by the stripes of Jesus, no disease
germ or virus has any place in their
bodies. Every tissue and every
organ in their bodies function to
perfection, which God created.
My grandchildren are healthy and
blessed of God.

SCRIPTURE

Proverbs 3:5-6

Trust in the Lord with all thine heart; and lean not unto your own understanding. In all thy ways acknowledge him, and he shall direct thy paths.

II Timothy 1:7

For God hath not given us the spirit of fear; but of power, and of love, and of a sound mind.

TRUST

My grandchildren are strong in the Lord and lean not to human understanding, but trust in God. The Lord is their strength and salvation. My children put their trust in God and fear is far from them.

SCRIPTURE

Galatians 5:22-23

But the fruit of the Spirit is love, joy, peace, longsuffering, gentleness, goodness, faith, meekness, temperance: against such there is no law.

FRUIT OF THE SPIRIT

My grandchildren are full of
love, joy, peace, longsuffering,
gentleness, goodness and faith.
The kingdom of God dwells in
them in righteousness, peace and
joy in the Holy Spirit.

CONFESSIONS

FOR

CHILDREN

SCRIPTURE

Psalms 118:29

"O give thanks unto the Lord; for he is good: for his mercy endureth for ever."

THANKSGIVING

I give thanks to God.

I thank you God, for my family.

I thank you God, for the Bible

I am thankful.

SCRIPTURE

Ephesians 4:32

"And be ye kind one to another, tenderhearted, forgiving one another, even as God for Christ's sake hath forgiven you."

KINDNESS

God is good and kind to me.

I am kind to others.

I forgive others.

The Love of God makes me kind.

SCRIPTURE

Matthew 22:37

"Jesus said unto him, Thou shalt love the Lord thy God with all thy heart, and with all thy soul, and with all thy mind."

LOVE

God loves me.

I love the Lord with all my heart.

I love the Lord with all my mind.

God's love is in my heart.

SCRIPTURE

Psalms 69:30

"I will praise the name of God with a song, and will magnify him with thanksgiving."

PRAISE

I think on good things.

I am full of praise.

I love to praise the Lord.

I will sing praises to God.

SCRIPTURE

Psalms 33:5

"He loveth righteousness and judgment: the earth is full of the goodness of the Lord."

BLESSING

I am a gift from God.

I am full of goodness.

God is good to me and

I am a blessing.

SCRIPTURE

Isaiah 12:2

*"Behold God is my salvation; I will trust, and not
be afraid: for the Lord JEHOVAH is my strength
and my song; he also is become my salvation."*

SAFETY

The angels watch over me.

God will satisfy me with long life.

I am obedient to God and His Word

And He keeps me safe.

SCRIPTURE

Colossians 3:20

"Children, obey your parents in all things: for this is well pleasing unto the Lord."

OBEDIENCE

I obey Jesus.

I am obedient to my parents.

I am willing and obedient.

I am blessed of God.

SCRIPTURE

I Peter 2:24

"Who his own self bare our sins in his own body on the tree, that we, being dead to sins, should live unto righteousness: by whose stripes ye were healed."

HEALING

God sent His Word and healed
me.

By Jesus' stripes I am healed.

I am healthy and blessed by God.

Sickness has no place in me.

SCRIPTURE

Proverbs 18:10

"The name of the Lord is a strong tower: the righteous runneth into it, and is safe."

TRUST

I will trust in the Lord, forever.

Jesus is my salvation.

I will trust in the Lord and not be afraid.

I am under God's protection.

SCRIPTURE

Romans 15:13

"Now the God of hope fill you with all joy and peace in believing, that ye may abound in hope, through the power of the Holy Ghost."

JOY

I have joy in my heart.

Jesus fills my life with joy.

I am full of love, joy, and peace.

I am a joyful child.

SALVATION PRAYER

Dear God, You loved the world so much, You gave Your only begotten Son to die for our sins so that whoever believes in Him will not perish, but have eternal life (John 3:16). Your word says that if I confess with my mouth and believe in my heart, I shall be saved, or born again (Romans 10:9-10). The Bible says we are saved by grace through faith as a gift from You. There is nothing I can do to earn salvation. I now confess Jesus as my Lord and Savior. Lord Jesus, I ask You to come into my heart and forgive me of my sins. I believe in my heart that You God raised Jesus from the dead so that I could be saved.

Thank You, Jesus for saving me. I am so grateful!

In Jesus' Name, Amen!

BOOKS BY BEVERLY CAPPS

THE THREE BEARS IN THE MINISTRY
THE THREE LITTLE PIGS
LITTLE RED RIDINGHOOD
LITTLE RED HEN
JACK AND THE BEANSTALK
CHICKEN LITTLE CONQUERS FEAR
SEEDTIME STORIES
HOW CAN I PLEASE YOU, GOD?
PRAYERS FOR PRE-SCHOOLERS
SHADRACH, MESHACH AND ABEDNEGO
DANIEL AND THE LIONS' DEN

GOD, ARE YOU REALLY REAL?
GOD IS MY BEST FRIEND
GOD IS NEVER TOO BUSY TO LISTEN
GOD LOVES MY TEDDY BEAR, TOO!
GOD HAS ALL THE ANSWERS
IS EASTER JUST FOR BUNNIES?

GOD'S CREATIVE POWER FOR BABIES AND TODDLERS
GOD'S CREATIVE POWER FOR PRESCHOOLERS
GOD'S CREATIVE POWER FOR KIDS
GOD'S CREATIVE POWER FOR GRANDPARENTs

VISIT US @ FAITHTALES.COM
1-800-388-5437
BEVERLY CAPPS MINISTRIES
BOX 69
ENGLAND, ARKANSAS 72046

Sunday School
Curriculum for Babies

Jesus Loves Me!

0 –12 Months

A complete year of lessons that minister to babies!

Organized and easy to use—even for the *first-time* teacher!

This set includes a sample of nursery policies and standards to use as a guide for organizing a church nursery. Help babies learn to recognize the Bible and Jesus. Teach them to recognize how much Jesus loves them! Fill the air around little ones with the love of God and His Word, planting an everlasting seed of faith! Flexible—begin *anytime!*

THIS SET INCLUDES:

* Master Lesson Book
* Teachers Instruction CD
* A Lullaby CD
* Poster of Jesus
* Baby Praise Book
* Master Set Reproducible Take-Home Papers
* One Bible
* Sample of Nursery Policies for Organization
* Two Children's Story Books by Beverly Capps:
  Prayers for Preschoolers
  How Can I Please You God?

$199.00

Samples available! See order form.

Sunday School
Curriculum for Toddlers

Jesus Loves Me, Too!

Toddlers from 12–24 Months

A complete year of lessons for toddlers.

This curriculum promotes the foundation of the authority of God's Word to change lives, w◣
focusing on Jesus Christ and our love for Him! Included is a full-bodied, stuffed, white bunny pup◣
that can be used to help toddlers learn to sing praise songs. The lovable bunny keeps interest al◣
Toddlers will develop a new awareness of Jesus and His goodness and will grow spiritually by
confession of God's Word over them!

THIS SET INCLUDES:

- Master Lesson Book
- Teacher's Instruction CD
- Full Bodied Stuffed Bunny Puppet
- Two Story Books by Beverly Capps:
  - Prayers for Preschoolers
  - How Can I Please You God?
- Poster of Jesus
- Baby Praise Book and CD
- Master Set Reproducible Take-Home Pap◣
- One Bible

$199.00 Samples available! See order form.

Curriculum for Ages 2-5

Friends With God

Preschoolers Ages 2-5

17 weeks of lessons

Organized and easy to use—even for the first-time teacher!

...aving a relationship with God is important for children. This planned-and-organized curriculum ...part of a series of teachings that will help children learn how to have a close trust in Him. It is ...rovided to help teachers train preschoolers to know that God is their best friend and that He ...ways will listen to them. In fact, He looks forward to it! *Nothing else to buy! You can start anytime ...uring the year.*

THIS SET INCLUDES:

* 17 Week Master Lesson Book
* Teacher's Instruction CD
* No-Mess Creative Wikki-Stix (two packages)
* "Gladly the Bear" Puppet
* Two Sheets Flannel Graph Characters
* Reproducible Coloring Sheets/Master Copies
* Three books:
  God Is Never Too Busy To Listen
  The Three Bears in the Ministry
  Little Red Ridinghood (retold as a faith tale)

$169.00   Samples available! See order form.

God's Word is Truth

Preschoolers Ages 2-5

17 weeks of lessons

Organized and easy to use—even for the first-time teacher!

This organized and easy-to-use curriculum is part of a series of teachings that will help childr build a relationship with God. It is provided to help teachers train preschoolers to know that Go Word is always truth, regardless of what might be going on around them! Having confiden enough to believe and rely on God's Word proves that a child has advanced his or her faith, a has strengthened his or her relationsip with God. *You can get started teaching preschoolers too with God's Word is Truth!*

THIS SET INCLUDES:

* 17 Week Master Lesson Book
* Teacher's Instruction CD
* No-Mess Creative Wikki-Stix (two packages)
* Coloring Sheets for Handout (reproducible)
* Duck Puppet (full size and soft)
* Two Sheets Flannel Graph Characters
* Three books:
  God, Are You Really Real?
  Jack and the Beanstalk (retold as a faith t
  Little Red Hen (retold as a faith tale)

$169.00

Samples available! See order form.

Obedience and Forgiveness

Preschoolers Ages 2-5

17 weeks of lessons

Organized and easy to use—even for the first-time teacher!

...hool children are not too young to learn how to have a good relationship with God. This good ...ionship depends on teaching them Bible stories, Bible principles, and elements of relationship. ...package is designed to teach preschoolers about obedience and forgiveness. *Everything you* *...to get started teaching preschoolers at anytime during the year.*

THIS SET INCLUDES:

* 17 Week Master Lesson Book
* Teacher's Instruction CD
* No-Mess Creative Wikki-Stix (two packages)
* Coloring Sheets for Handout (reproducible)
* Benji Bunny Puppet
* 2 Sheets of Flannel Graph Characters
* Three books:
  Chicken Little Conquers Fear
  The Three Little Pigs
     (Building Your House Upon a Rock)
  God Is My Best Friend

$169.00   Samples available! See order form.

Faith Building

Curriculum for Ages 6-12

Mighty Through God

Children Ages 6-12

17 weeks of lessons

Understanding God's power teaches children to have reverent fear of Almighty God; or in other w
understanding His power is key to their having respect for Him. To help build this kind of rever
toward God, this curriculum helps children learn the character of God by studying the names of
When children know God's character, they build a closer relationship with Him.

Children involved in this curriculum will also study Bible stories of men of God and how they re
to Him. Through these stories, children will learn about God's awesome power and His ability to
on our behalf. Children will learn that He is our loving Father, but He is also Almighty God, Jeho

This faith-building curriculum is organized and easy to use, regardless of the teacher's level of exper

*Children will learn the names of the boc
the New Testament, all in order by th
of the this curriculum. You can
any time of the*

THIS SET INCLUDES:

* 17 Week Master Lesson Book
* Master Set of Reproducible Activity S
* Master Set of Reproducible Coloring S
* Two Books:
   Daniel and the Lions' Den
   Seedtime Stories

$137.50   Samples available! See order form.